NATIONAL GEOGRAPHIC
School Publishing

Figuras

Edward Lincoln

PICTURE CREDITS

Illustration by Marjory Gardner (14–15).

Cover, 2, 4 (above), 5 (center & right), 6 (all), 7 (all), 8 (below right), 9 (all), 10 (left), 11 (below left & above right), 12 (left), Photolibrary.com; 1, 4 (below), 5 (below), Lindsay Edwards Photography; 4 (center), Swerve/Alamy; 5 (above left), Zefa Images; 8 (left), 11 (above left), 12 (below right), 13 (above left, above right & below), Getty Images; 8 (above right), Photodisc.

Produced through the worldwide resources of the National Geographic Society, John M. Fahey, Jr., President and Chief Executive Officer; Gilbert M. Grosvenor, Chairman of the Board.

PREPARED BY NATIONAL GEOGRAPHIC SCHOOL PUBLISHING

Ericka Markman, Senior Vice President and President Children's Books and Education Publishing Group; Steve Mico, Senior Vice President and Publisher; Marianne Hiland, Editorial Director; Lynnette Brent, Executive Editor; Michael Murphy and Barbara Wood, Senior Editors; Bea Jackson, Design Director; David Dumo, Art Director; Margaret Sidlowsky, Illustrations Director; Matt Wascavage, Manager of Publishing Services; Sean Philpotts, Production Manager.

SPANISH LANGUAGE VERSION PREPARED BY
NATIONAL GEOGRAPHIC SCHOOL PUBLISHING GROUP

Sheron Long, CEO; Sam Gesumaria, President; Fran Downey, Vice President and Publisher; Margaret Sidlosky, Director of Design and Illustrations; Paul Osborn, Senior Editor; Sean Philpotts, Project Manager; Lisa Pergolizzi, Production Manager.

MANUFACTURING AND QUALITY MANAGEMENT

Christopher A. Liedel, Chief Financial Officer; George Bounelis, Vice President; Clifton M. Brown III, Director.

BOOK DEVELOPMENT

Ibis for Kids Australia Pty Limited.

SPANISH LANGUAGE TRANSLATION

Tatiana Acosta/Guillermo Gutiérrez

SPANISH LANGUAGE BOOK DEVELOPMENT

Navta Associates, Inc.

Published by the National Geographic Society
Washington, D.C. 20036-4688

ISBN: 978-0-7362-3838-0

Printed in the United States of America

19 18 17 16 15

10 9 8 7 6 5 4

Contenido

dianas

boleto

círculo

rectángulo

cuadrado

4

¿Qué figuras ven en estas fotografías?

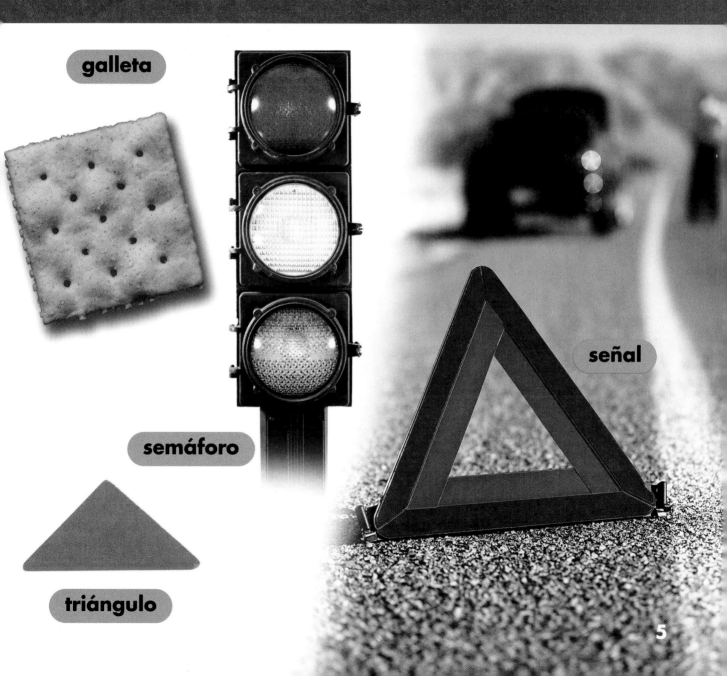

galleta

semáforo

triángulo

señal

Círculos

Un círculo es una figura redonda.

Triángulos ▲ ▼

Un triángulo tiene 3 lados rectos y 3 esquinas.

Rectángulos

Un rectángulo tiene 4 lados rectos y 4 esquinas.

Cuadrados

Un cuadrado es un rectángulo especial.
Sus 4 lados tienen el mismo largo.

14

círculo

cuadrado

esquina

figura

lado

rectángulo

redonda

triángulo

Glosario ilustrado

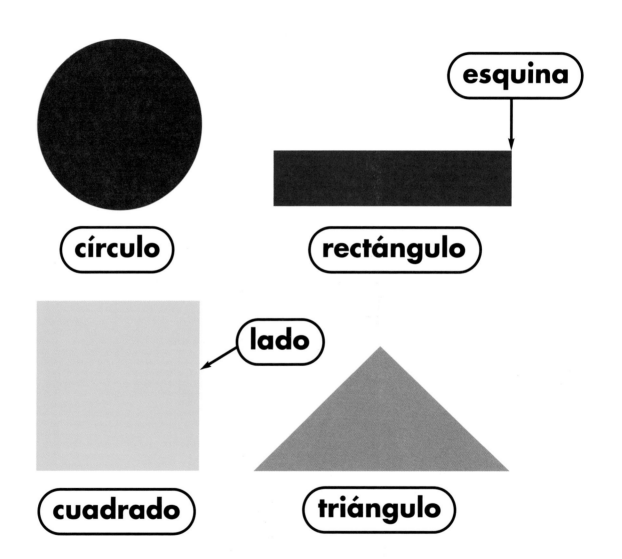

círculo

esquina

rectángulo

lado

cuadrado

triángulo